(Don't)
Follow the Herd

AₚP™
Acclaim Press
MORLEY, MISSOURI

(Don't) Follow the Herd

7 Costly Mistakes People Make with Their Money

...and How to Avoid Them

Tony Walker

Acclaim Press
—— *Your Next Great Book* ——
P.O. Box 238
Morley, MO 63767
(573) 472-9800
www.acclaimpress.com

Library of Congress Cataloging-in-Publication Data

Walker, Tony, 1960-
  Don't follow the herd / by Tony Walker.
    p. cm.
  ISBN-13: 978-1-935001-43-0 (alk. paper)
  ISBN-10: 1-935001-43-4 (alk. paper)
  1. Finance, Personal. I. Title.
  HG179.W3125 2010
  332.024--dc22

                                    2010009794

Third Printing: 2010
Printed in the United States of America
10 9 8 7 6

Contents

Tony's Talk Begins 15

The Story of Wally World 27

Wally Meets Farmer Brown 41

Wally Learns It's Not About the Money 65

The Workshop Attendees Respond 85

Tony Explains the 7 Costly Mistakes People Make

    with Their Money 89

Tony Wraps It Up 139

Notes 142

Other Resources by Tony Walker 143

This little book is written for Savers.

It is dedicated to those who are tired of drinking downstream from the rest of the Financial Herd. The content is a result of personally speaking and visiting with thousands of hard-working Americans who, over my past 25 years in the financial world, have been courageous enough to share with me their true hopes and dreams about themselves, their loved ones and their money.

It is my sincere hope this book will reveal the truth about your money and expose the methods used by the financial world who keep chasing after it.

Finally, and most importantly, that the simple story within these pages might help you to discover, as I have, that our brief stay on earth is "not about the money."

Be Worryfree!

Tony Walker
America's MoneyMissionary®

"For the gate is wide, and the way is broad that leads to destruction, and many are those who find it."

Matthew 7:13

(Don't) Follow the Herd

7 Costly Mistakes People Make with Their Money

...and How to Avoid Them

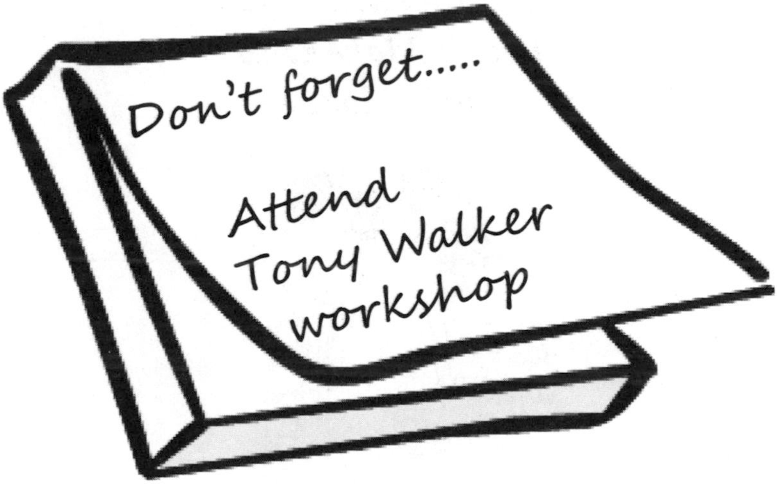
Don't forget.....
Attend
Tony Walker
workshop

Tony's Talk Begins

"Welcome, folks, to tonight's educational workshop entitled, 'How to Make Millions of Dollars Without Ever Lifting a Finger.'"

{People in the crowd look at each other as if they're in the wrong workshop.}

"Just kidding," quips Tony.

"I'm Tony Walker, author and creator of the Worry-Free Retirement®, and tonight I'll be sharing with you the Seven Costly Mistakes people make with their money and how you can avoid them."

{Audience looks relieved upon realizing they're in the right place.}

"For twenty-five years, I've provided financial advice to all types of people on all sorts of financial issues. I've worked with rich people, poor people and people in between, and over all those years of working in the financial trenches, here's what I've discovered: no matter how much money you save, invest or speculate with—no matter whether you've made boat-loads of money, or lost a ton of it—when it comes to making money, the Financial World always seems to come out on top."

{Crowd nods in agreement.}

"Why might that be?"

{Tony waits for a response.}

"Because the Financial World knows how to make money with our money," shouts a middle-aged man in the back row.

"Because the financial advisors who work for them never explain things in terms that I can understand," says a senior citizen in the front row.

"So, if that's the case," responds Tony, "why do many hard-working Americans continue to blindly invest their money with them?"

"What in the heck are we supposed to do?" chimes a man in the far corner. "I mean, it's either hand over our money or bury it in the backyard, which lately, I've been thinking might not be such a bad idea."

{Crowd laughs in agreement.}

"Even though I've lost a bunch of money in the stock market," says a female voice from the audience, "my advisor keeps telling me to just 'hang in there.'"

"And how do you feel about their advice?" asks Tony.

"I'm sixty years old…I don't have time to hang in there," she responds in an even more exasperated tone.

"Tonight," as Tony turns to the next slide, "you will learn why the Financial World always seems to come out on top, regardless of whether 'we' do or not. You will leave with new ideas and proven strategies on how you can gain more control of your money by NOT following the herd."

{Many of the participants begin taking notes}

"Isn't that why," Tony continues, "all of you took time out of your busy schedules to come to this workshop: so you can learn how to better use, enjoy and protect your money?"

"Now you're talkin' Sonny," says a jubilant, older fellow sitting up front. "What I want to know is when in the h-e-double-hockey sticks can I start enjoying some of this money I've been savin' all my life?"

{Everyone laughs out loud.}

{With the crowd fully engaged, Tony slowly turns and walks behind his overhead projector. He begins to draw a picture of a highway as he continues to explain his point.}

"Imagine you—and a herd of hundreds of other cars and trucks—are speeding together down Interstate 65. You're driving eighty miles per hour for two reasons: first, because everybody else is and second, if you don't, the rest of the herd will run over you!"

"Been there done that," quips a voice from the crowd.

"Okay, so there you are, racing along with this herd of cars when all of a sudden, the radio announcer reports that the bridge ahead has just collapsed and that cars are plunging hundreds of feet into the Ohio River. You—and all the other clueless drivers around you—are heading straight for disaster!"

"What do you do?"

"Get off on the nearest exit…what do you think I'd do?" shouts a serious minded older lady toward the back of the room.

{Everyone shouts "Amen."}

"Okay," says Tony, "but what if every other car around you kept driving full speed ahead? What if you were the only one who heard the radio report? Or worse yet, what if the radio announcer had his wires crossed and the bridge really wasn't out? Would you still break away from the herd of cars and get off the interstate, possibly losing valuable time for nothing? Or, would you stay with the herd, trusting they knew what they were doing?"

{The crowd remains silent until somebody speaks up.}

"What you're saying is sometimes it's just easier to follow the herd," shouts a voice.

{Tony nods and continues.}

"The story you're about to hear resembles decisions that you and I make each and every day. It's a story of human nature; why we do certain things and follow certain people when, deep down inside, we know we shouldn't. *Don't Follow the Herd* tells the story of a well-meaning young man representing the Financial World and a chance encounter he has with a Cow Farmer. My hope is that by the end of this short story, you'll have a better understanding of how the Financial World so easily leads us astray."

"Get on with it, Sonny…we don't have all night!" shouts an older fellow in the front row.

The Story of Wally World

Once upon a time, far away in a very big city, there lived a well-mannered, very energetic and talkative young lad by the name of Wally World.

Wally is so talkative that his fifth grade teacher, Terri Tutor, tells Wally he could possibly be suffering from a condition known as HVN. Wally later discovers that HVN stands for "High Verbal Needs."

Wally's grandmother just calls it "the gift of gab!"

Ms. Tutor likes Wally and wants him to be happy and successful. One day, she encourages Wally to apply his well-mannered, energetic personality—and HVN—and become a teacher. She tells Wally that teaching will put his unique gifts on "center stage" so that he can help others. Wally likes the idea of being on center stage and helping others.

Wally's father, Tuff, works day and night to provide for the World Family. Tuff and his wife, Faith, never attended college because their parents couldn't afford it. Tuff and Faith desperately want Wally to get a college degree so that Wally won't have to work so hard to make ends meet.

Sitting at the kitchen table one night, Wally remembers his dad saying, "Wally, in order to avoid going to The Poor House, you'll need a good, college education."

Wally's parents want the best for Wally. Wally does, too!

So after years of 60-hour work weeks and stashing away every extra red cent they could find, Tuff and Faith finally saved enough money to afford tuition to one of the most prestigious University's in the country: High & Mighty University. Otherwise known as HMU.

The graduation line at HMU is crowded with young adults of all ages, shapes and sizes. Anxious to receive his diploma, Wally slowly follows the long line of students in front of him. Tuff always says, "When your last name begins with 'W', you get used to following the herd."

After what seems like hours, Wally finally arrives at the steps leading up to the big stage where the President of High & Mighty University, Timmy Tuition, stands. President Tuition waits at center stage, personally greeting each student with his or her very own college diploma. Finally, it is Wally's turn to receive his diploma!

Walking across the stage toward President Tuition, Wally begins to feel his stomach churn as all eyes focus on him. Slowly approaching the massive podium where President Tuition stands, Wally now feels the warmth and glow of the stage lights focused on the podium. For a brief moment, Wally feels as if the President—and the thousands of people in attendance—are there just to see Wally get his diploma. For the first time in his life, Wally is on center stage.

And then, just when things can't seem to get any better, Wally hears the following announcement booming throughout the vast auditorium's loud speakers:

With the entire graduating class now seated, a distinguished gentleman, dressed in a well-pressed pinstripe suit, approaches the podium previously occupied by President Tuition. To the surprise of everyone in attendance, it is the city's wealthiest man, the owner of World Financial, Marty Millionaire. Marty Millionaire is so well-respected that people say, "when Marty speaks, people listen."

In fact, Marty Millionaire is so famous that the prestigious *Financial World Magazine* had featured Marty on its cover. The picture of Mr. Millionaire sitting "center stage" on the balcony of his penthouse high atop the Financial World Building left a lasting impression on Wally. Wally would give anything to be in the spotlight like that.

"Ladies and gentlemen," announces Marty Million-

aire. "I congratulate each and every one of you on graduating from HMU. However, just because you have a college degree doesn't mean you'll be successful like me. In fact, some of you will still end up in The Poor House."

Wally is shocked! One of the world's most successful men just told hundreds of college graduates that they could still end up in The Poor House. Anxious to hear more, Wally leans forward in his chair.

"The secret to staying out of the Poor House," Mr. Millionaire continues, "is to figure out how to get OPM."

"OPM?" Wally asks himself. Wally had HVN, but OPM? He'd never heard of such a condition…

Mr. Millionaire's voice becomes even more deliberate as he repeats himself: "That's OPM—Other People's Money."

A feeling of sadness falls upon Wally. Wally had always been led to believe that having HVN was the secret to success. But now, after four grueling years of college, one of the wealthiest men in the world is saying that the secret to success was something called OPM, a condition Wally has never heard of and isn't sure how to get.

"But let not your hearts be troubled," continues Marty Millionaire. "As I speak, The Financial World is hiring young, energetic college graduates who would like to stay out of The Poor House. In fact, we're especially interested in hiring young men and women who have a condition known as HVN."

"Whoo-Hooo," shouts Wally.

Wally Meets Farmer Brown

Ten years have passed since Wally's graduation from HMU. His wife, Willa — along with their two wonderful children, Goody and Woody — enjoy a big home, nice cars and attend the best private schools money can buy. Friends, family and clients admire the World's successful lifestyle.

But Wally knows better.

Mortgaged to the hilt and running on his last nickel, Wally and his fellow Financial World Representatives have been led to believe that "acting successful" is the secret to finding OPM. Wally had taken the bait hook, line and sinker. Mr. Millionaire had made getting OPM sound so easy. Wally had "acted" the part of success, but now it was time to pay up.

Wally thinks that things couldn't get worse until late one afternoon, following a long and grueling eight hours of "dialing for dollars" (that's what Wally's sales manager used to call it), Wally's worst nightmare came true: Marty Millionaire wants to see Wally in his office — NOW.

As Wally cautiously approaches the luxurious office of Mr. Millionaire, he notices a humongous leather chair located behind the most beautiful mahogany desk Wally had ever seen. As Wally approaches the desk, the chair slowly turns around to reveal a very relaxed Marty Millionaire, who plainly says: "Wally, if you don't hurry up and find me OPM, you're going to find yourself without a J.O.B."

Wally leaves work that day with fear and panic. Instead of taking the usual route home, Wally—along with hundreds of other cars—continues driving down Interstate 65. Worried that his family was heading to The Poor House, Wally glances into the rearview mirror to see the big city growing smaller. The thought of driving away from it all seems appealing to Wally. So, he just keeps driving.

As Wally merges off the busy Interstate and away from the big city, he soon finds himself navigating the unfamiliar country road of Highway 33. The sight of the peaceful pastures, dotted with farmhouses and pretty red barns, helps alleviate Wally's worries.

After several hours of driving the scenic route, Wally notices a peculiar site in a distant pasture. From what he can tell, it appeared to be a large herd of cows slowly walking along behind a lone man.

Curious to get a closer look, Wally immediately turns his shiny, red sports car off Highway 33 and onto a dirt road leading toward the herd of cows.

With dust trailing behind, Wally slowly drives toward the large herd of cattle before coming to a complete stop. The older man leading the herd is wearing bibbed overalls and carrying a small milk bucket. As Wally's car came to a stop, the man and his herd turn in the direction of Wally. The older gentleman begins walking toward Wally, and the cows curiously stare in the direction of this stranger in the little red sports car.

As Wally steps from the car, he notices a large truck parked by a big red barn in the direction of where the man and the cows are heading. The truck is clearly marked with large black letters that read: "Chuck's Slaughterhouse."

Walking toward the herd of cows are at least a dozen men dressed in blue jeans, cowboy boots and hats. The men are prodding several of the cows—apparently encouraging them to move toward the big ramp that lead into the rear of the truck. Wally also notices a man, similar in age to Wally, exiting the front door of a nearby farmhouse. The young man smiles and waves to Wally. Wally smiles and waves back.

"Howdy," says the older gentleman as he holds the milk bucket in one hand and extends the other toward Wally.

Wally accepts the farmer's hand as the two begin a firm, yet friendly handshake. Although the farmer is up in years, Wally is surprised by the strength of the farmer's grip.

"What are you doing with all those cows?" asks Wally as the farmer releases the tight grip on Wally's hand.

"Who wants to know?" says the farmer.

"Oh, I'm sorry. My name is Wally...Wally World. I live in the big city."

"Oh, a City Slicker. Could tell from them soft hands; like you been workin' behind a desk all your life," the older man says with a sly grin. "My name is Farmer Brown."

"Nice to meet you Mr. Brown...may I ask you a nosey question?"

"All depends."

At this point, Wally and the older gentleman begin slowly walking toward the cows, with some of the cows being herded into Chuck's Slaughterhouse truck, most continuing their curious gaze at this out-of-place City Slicker.

"How in the world are you able to get all those cows to follow you like that?"

"Them cows?" responds Farmer Brown as he looks over his shoulder at the huge herd. "I just tap on this here milk bucket and they follow. Once them cows get a taste of what's in this bucket, I can get them to go just about anywhere."

"I see," responds Wally. "And who are those fellows herding the cows into the truck?"

"Well," says Farmer Brown, "the young buck comin' out of the farmhouse there is my son, Junior. Them other fellas over there herdin' the cows are called Cowboys. I call em' my hired help. Their job is to get all them cows herded into ole' Chuck's truck so he can get em' over to his Slaughterhouse so I can make some money."

"What happens once the cows get to Chuck's Slaughterhouse?" asks Wally.

"Boy, you are a City Slicker, aren't ya?" asks Farmer Brown. "Let's just say that after they go to Chuck's, their next stop is the great cow pasture in the sky."

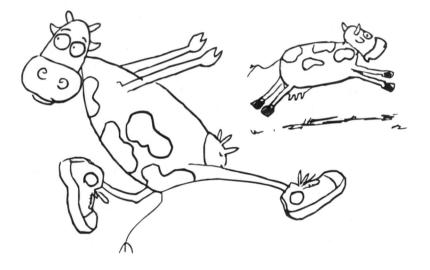

Wally, trying to hold back his confusion, continues with another question. "Do the cows ever try to get away?"

"Oh, ever once in a while you'll have a cow break away from the herd, but we always catch her. That's why we brand em'! Let's everybody knows who's boss—who owns the cows. It also let's me keep track with how much money I'm a makin'."

A light bulb goes off as Wally excitedly asks, "do you think there's much difference between cows and people?"

"Heck, I've always said in some ways, cows and people are a lot alike."

"Well Farmer Brown, it's obvious you know how to make money with cows. Problem is, I'm having a difficult time figuring out how to make money off people. My job is to try to herd people's money into the financial world… my boss calls it OPM."

"Other People's Money?" asks Farmer Brown.

"You know about OPM?" a stunned Wally responds.

"Sonny, how do you think I've been so successful at raisin' cows?"

"But, with all due respect, Mr. Brown, you don't look successful; what with your little house over there and that beat up old red barn," says Wally.

"Wally," says a suspecting Farmer Brown, "most City Slickers I meet suffer from BHNC. You wouldn't be one of em' would ya'?"

"What's BHNC?" responds Wally.

"Big Hat – No Cattle!" exclaims Farmer Brown.

{Wally continues to look intently at Farmer Brown for an explanation}

"Wally, just because a man's got a bunch of stuff — fancy cars, nice home and spiffy clothes — doesn't mean he's got any money. That's what I mean by Big Hat – No Cattle."

"Farmer Brown," says Wally in a serious tone, "All I know is if I don't find my boss some OPM, me and my family are heading for The Poor House. Surely, there's some wisdom you can share with me to convince people to follow what I'm saying."

{The two men continue to look at each other for a few moments as Farmer Brown thinks about Wally's predicament}

"There's an ole' saying, says Farmer Brown, "never drink downstream from the rest of the herd."

"With all due respect Farmer Brown, now I'm really confused!"

"Wally – all you gotta do is convince people that the water they're drinkin' is supposed to taste funny. What they don't know, won't hurt em'…get it?"

"Whoo-hoo," shouts Wally.

Quicker than you can say, "OPM," Wally quickly turns and begins a fast pace in the direction of his shiny, red sports car. With this new-found wisdom of people and cows, Wally is sure that his chance encounter with Farmer Brown will lead to tremendous success in finding OPM.

As Wally climbs into his car and turns the key to the ignition, he hears Farmer Brown shout, "Remember, Wally, cows are cows and people are people. Don't ever confuse the two."

Upon arriving at Financial World Incorporated head-quarters, Wally makes a mad dash to his second floor cubicle. Climbing into the small chair within his cramped cubicle, with pen and paper in hand, Wally quickly takes notes as his mind races....

How to Convince People to Follow the Herd
By Wally World

1. Give them a taste of what they like and keep banging on the bucket
2. Show them the pretty truck – never the ugly slaughter house (long-term bar chart of ever increasing returns vs. short term- dalbar vs. actual)
3. Brand them with your name - use the cattle prod if necessary.
4. Never forget how the hired help get paid.
5. Convince them that the milk is more important than the cow
6. Never teach them the difference between the good hay and the bad (good debt bad debt)
7. Don't remind them how fat they're getting or they might want to shed some weight.

Wally Learns It's Not About the Money

After thirty years of gathering OPM for the Financial World, Wally replaces Marty Millionaire as the Financial World's most successful advisor.

All around the Financial World, people are now saying, "when Wally speaks, people listen."

With the help of Farmer Brown, Wally had narrowly escaped the dreaded Poor House. It was a dream come true for Wally and Willa, because now they occupied the plush Penthouse formerly owned by Marty Millionaire (who had gone on to that big, financial cow pasture in the sky). Wally was truly on center stage!

It was a clear, crisp Saturday morning. Wally and Willa relaxed on the penthouse balcony with their morning cup of coffee, watching the sun rise over the nearby skyscrapers. With Wally sitting pretty at the top of the World, you'd think he wouldn't have a care in the world. But on this particular morning, Willa can sense that Wally is deeply preoccupied, almost as if troubled by something.

"Wally?" asks Willa, "what's bothering you?"

"Willa, after all these years of success, there has been something nagging me. Something that Farmer Brown said some thirty years ago that I've never understood."

{There's a moment of silence as Wally gathers his thoughts while Willa listens.}

"He said, 'cows are cows and people are people—don't ever confuse the two.'"

"But Wally," responds Willa, "Farmer Brown's advice was the reason we stayed out of The Poor House—you said so yourself. Why, after all of these years, would you question that?"

"Because I've always felt somewhat guilty about the way I convinced all those people to follow the herd," says Wally. "I just don't feel content with how I made all of this money by using OPM...if this is what it feels like being on Center Stage, I'm not so sure I want any part of it," he says as his voice trails off.

{Willa continues to gaze at Wally, waiting for a better explanation.}

"I guess," continues Wally, "I'll never know why Farmer Brown took the time to share so much about cows, yet reminded me that cows aren't people. It's as if he was trying to warn me about something."

"Wally?"

"Yes, dear…"

"You always trained your Junior Executives (Wally called them his "hired help") never to put off tomorrow what you could do today, right?"

"Yes, of course dear," as Wally continues to stare into the sunrise.

"Do you really believe that?" asks Willa.

Wally's attention suddenly turned to Willa as he pondered her question. "What do you mean, dear?" he asks.

"Wally," Willa plainly states, "get in your car and go ask Farmer Brown what he meant!"

It was a beautiful day as Wally drives his brand-new, four-door shiny sedan along scenic Highway 33. Wally had always believed that meeting Farmer Brown some thirty years ago was fate – a stroke of luck. But now, all these years later, for all Wally knows, Farmer Brown has since sold his cattle operation and moved on to greener pastures.

After several hours of driving, Wally spots the familiar turn in the road leading down toward the narrow two-lane bridge. As Wally hurries his car toward the bridge, he can see the same cliff rising high above the road. And, wouldn't you know it…walking over the cliff, away from Wally, is a huge herd of cows led by a lone man wearing bibbed overalls.

Anxious to visit with Farmer Brown again, Wally quickly drives over the narrow bridge, making a quick, hard-left turn off Highway 33 and onto the dirt road leading up the steep hill toward the distant figures. A trail of dust follows Wally's shiny 4-door sedan as he surveys the slightly overgrown, yet still familiar terrain of Farmer Brown's old place.

What a thrill it will be for Wally to visit with his old friend once again.

"Hello," announces Wally as he quickly exits his car and walks toward the farmer. "I've been anxious to see you to ask you...."

{Wally's voice trails off realizing that the man in bibbed overalls is not Farmer Brown.}

"Howdy!" responds the farmer. "What can I do ya' for?"

"My name is Wally World. I've driven a long way trying to find a fellow by the name of Farmer Br..."

The farmer abruptly interrupts Wally, while at the same time, extends his hand to shake Wally's, "I remember you."

"Wait a minute," a shocked Wally exclaims, "you're Farmer Brown's son, Junior."

"Yep."

"Well, it's good to see you. How the heck are you?"

"Looks like somebody's moved up in the world," as Junior eyes Wally's new 4-door sedan.

"Oh, yeah, thanks," says a surprised Wally. "Where's your dad? I really need to ask him something."

"Wally," Junior responds as he turns his attention back to Wally, "my father's dead."

"He's dead?" a shocked Wally responds.

"Don't look so dog-gone sad Wally. As Pa always said, everybody's gonna kick the bucket sometime. I mean, I miss him and all, but my dad had a good life. He got a kick out of herdin' cows and helpin' people; somethin' he loved doin'. Not many men can say that!"

"Yeah," says Wally, "I always admired the way he used all those cows to make money. He certainly taught me a great deal about using OPM to become successful."

"Now hold on to your cowbell there a minute Wally; my dad was a good businessman and all, but he never felt like he was usin' them cows. To him, raisin' cows wasn't about the money."

"It wasn't?" responds a confused Wally.

"Heck no. It was about the people."

"What people?" a now very confused Wally asks.

75

"All the people my dad provided for all them years," continues Farmer Brown, Jr. "Me, my mom, the hired help over there, all the employees of Chuck's Slaughterhouse, and most of all, City Slickers like you who got to eat and enjoy all those good steaks and hamburgers…that's what it was about Wally."

Wally's face grows more serious as he slowly bows his head and stares at the dirt road. He is sad to hear of the loss of Farmer Brown. With the death of Farmer Brown, the meaning of his last words to Wally will forever remain a mystery. Wally's head hangs down as he begins to return to his car.

"He told me you'd be comin' back here some day," shouts Junior.

{Wally stops and turns back to Junior with a puzzled look.}

"My dad took a likin' to you Wally. Said you'd come back here when you figured out what he meant when he told you 'cows are cows and people are people — don't ever confuse the two.'"

"How did you know that's what he told me?"

"That was his favorite saying."

Frustrated, Wally raises his voice slightly, "What did he mean by that?"

"Believe it or not, Pa loved them cows. He treated em' well. He made sure that they was kept out of bad weather, kept em' fed well and took care of them when they was sick. But he knew they was just cows—not people."

"But the cows—they all end up in the slaughterhouse, right?" Wally says. "Wasn't Farmer Brown just fattening them up and herding them all over these pastures so he could make a bunch of money from them?"

"A bunch of money…are you kiddin', Wally? There were years when Pa had to borrow against the farm just to keep it all goin'. He wanted to do something for people and these cows were just a way to do that. Now, even though my father's dead, I can continue to do the same thing. And in a few years, I hope my boy will want to carry on the good work of raisin' cows and helpin' people. Because that's what life's all about."

As Wally climbs into his shiny four-door sedan, he can see the hired help loading one cow after another into Chuck's Slaughterhouse truck. For the first time in his life, Wally finally understood what Farmer Brown meant by "cows are cows and people are people—don't ever confuse the two."

Wally smiled at Junior, and with a friendly wave and a nod of his head, slowly drove his car down the dirt road leading to Highway 33. Wally's mind raced back to graduation day from HMU—Marty Millionaire was wrong. Life wasn't about OPM. It wasn't about the money. It was about the people. True contentment isn't found in herding people around like cattle, but rather, it is about treating them with dignity and respect.

Cows are cows, and people are people, and Wally would never confuse the two again.

The Workshop Attendees Respond

The crowd remains silent until a young man in the middle of the room blurts, "I don't get it?"

"I think I do," responds an older lady in the front row.

"So what's the story about?" Tony asks the lady.

"Well, it's obvious that with the help of Farmer Brown, Wally figured out how to get OPM. But toward the end of his life, he was troubled by the way he got it. It's like, even though Wally was very successful, he was never content."

{Tony waits for more feedback}

"I guess he's no different than anybody else," comments a smartly dressed man seated to Tony's left. "There's always that fine line between working hard to stay out of The Poor House and doing what's right in order to make money – like herding people around like cattle."

"One thing you must understand," continues Tony, "is that the Financial World has every right to try and sell you on their services and products; to convince you to follow them – it's called Capitalism. And as long as it's on the up-and-up, that's perfectly okay and legal. But never forget whose money this is…it's yours! It is your responsibility to learn the rules of The Financial World so you won't be blindly led astray. Remember what Farmer Brown told Wally, "never drink downstream from the rest of the herd."

{The crowd all nods in agreement.}

"So how do we stop following the herd?" asks a younger man seated to Tony's right.

"Yeah," says another young lady sitting beside him. "I don't want to follow the herd. I want to learn what's best for me and my family!"

"That's the spirit, says Tony. "Let's all get out your workbooks and go through the seven costly mistakes people make with their money."

"Ready?"

"Get on with it, sonny," responds an elderly man in the front row, "we don't have all night!"

The 7 Costly Mistakes
People Make with Their Money

Mistake Number 1
Paying Taxes on the Same Dollar More Than Once

It has been said that great mastermind, Albert Einstein, once referred to compound interest as the "eighth wonder of the world." If that's true, then obviously ole' Albert never lived under our nation's present tax system!

You see, in the U.S. of A., we are guided by what the politicians affectionately refer to as a "progressive" tax system. Simply put: "the more we make, the more they take!"

Nevertheless, most Americans are following the herd in thinking that "compound interest" is a good thing––and it would be if we lived in a perfect "tax-free" world. But we don't.

Certificates of Deposits (CD), Taxable Bonds, Mutual Funds, Real Estate, Money Markets and individual Stocks (just to name a few) can certainly grow (compound) to sizeable amounts of cash. The problem is, as most of these accounts grow and compound, so does the Government's fair share—called Taxes!

Let me show you what I mean…

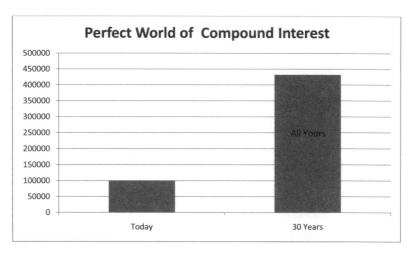

As you can see, the growth of the CD at 5%, compounded over the course of time, is quite "magical" indeed!

But hold on to your branding iron because the government has something to say about all this magical compounding. With any kind of growth, it now becomes your "patriotic duty" to share the "magic" with the I.R.S. – even if this means paying taxes on money that's already been taxed (not a good thing).

But the nightmare is not over. Take a look at what happens to the money (the taxes due on our money) that is now "gone forever" into the government rat hole.

You see, whenever we have a cost (taxes each year) we

Real World of Taxes

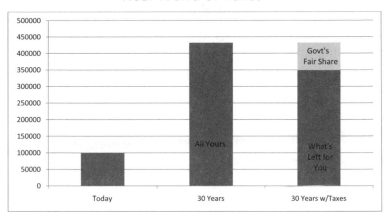

also create another wealth eroding problem called Lost Opportunity Cost, or LOC.

LOC simply implies that whenever you and I incur a cost, i.e. taxes, insurance premiums, interest, fees, etc., we not only lose the dollar, we lose the interest we could have earned had we avoided the cost. The effects of LOC on our illustration reveal the "horror" of compounding interest; especially, in a taxable account…

How do you avoid all of these taxes and LOC?

Real World of Taxes and LOC

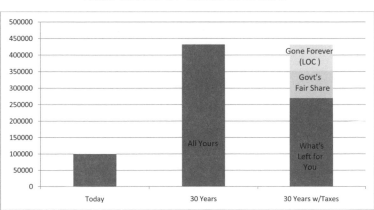

Two options: you find financial products and strategies (we'll talk later about these) that allow you to defer the taxes (thus eliminating the LOC) or you deal with the original tax up front and avoid future taxes altogether.

Bottom line: be sure you are working with an advisor who can help monitor your taxes each year. By lowering taxes you are also lowering LOC, which in turn gives you more money to use and enjoy at no additional risk or out of pocket expenses to you.

Mistake Number 2
Walking by Blind Faith

The date: October 9, 2007. The Dow is at an all time high: 14,164. Frustrated with low CD rates, Joe Lunchbox (who considers himself conservative – a saver) is one unhappy camper. Over the years, ole' Joe enjoyed decent interest rates from his FDIC bank products, but on this particular day, a chance encounter with Wally World convinces Joe to change course by closing out his "safe stuff" and moving his $100,000 retirement account at the bank into a "diversified" portfolio (with Wally's company) of growth mutual funds.

Well, as the old saying goes: "what goes up must come down."

And down Joe went...along with much of his life savings.

Frustrated by the quick drop, Joe calls Wally for solutions. Wally confidently informs Joe that there are now only two options: "hang in there" and wait for the market to come back up; or secondly, get out of the market and take his losses. Joe hangs up the phone and is back to being an unhappy camper. Since Joe doesn't want to take his losses, he asks Wally how much the account will have to grow in order to get back to break even. To which Wally replies, "Who knows?"

I know, so let's take a look...

Date of Investment: October 9, 2007
DOW at the time: 14,164
Amount invested: $100,000
Type account: Taxable Mutual fund
Tax Bracket: 33%
Assumed loss: 40%

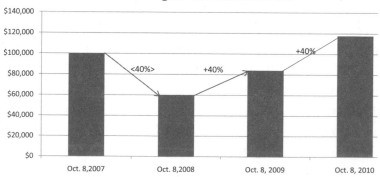

As the chart illustrates, even if Joe's growth mutual

funds, which previously dropped by 40%, grow by 40% each year (which is highly unlikely), it still takes nearly three years (when you include the 40% loss, taxes and LOC) of earning 40% per year to get back to his original principal of $100,000!

Repeat: Joe's account would have to grow by over 40% PER YEAR, for nearly three years in a row, to get back to his original savings of $100,000.

How discouraging is that?

Let's summarize Joe's blind walk of faith and who really benefited:

1. Joe loses all hope of retiring Worry Free.

2. Joe loses a lot of sleep (we'll talk about Sleep Insurance later).

3. Regardless of whether Joe makes money or not, Wally still gets his fair share, via fees off of Joe's account (Wally loves fees).

4. Regardless of whether Joe makes money or not, Uncle Sam still gets his fair share (even though Joe lost money) via taxes on the account.

Think we could franchise this deal?

And while we're talking about cattle calling (how to herd people and their money) let's look at another one of Wally's favorite tactics: "average rate of return" vs. "real rate of return."

Column B shows $10,000 of Joe Lunchbox's piddly account at the bank (Wally's terminology to describe Joe's FDIC-insured CD) compared to Wally's proposed growth mutual fund (column A). Take note as to the "average return" mentioned by Wally of the past performance of this particular mutual fund at 6.7% (again, don't get up in arms here – it's just an example). Now, take a look at the "actual" return of this fund: 4.83%. Not too impressive when you realize that it is the exact same return as the safe and secure CD with its piddly interest rate of 4.83.

YEAR	WALLY (A)	JOE LUNCHBOX (B)
1	+20%	+4.83%
2	+20%	+4.83%
3	-20%	+4.83%
	_____	_____
Average Rate of Return	+6.7%	+4.83%
Actual Yield	+4.83%	+4.83%
	_____	_____
Net Amount in Pocket	$11,520	$11,520

Now that's very interesting…Joe would have just as much money had he left it in the safer pastures of his local bank.

Which pasture would you feel more comfortable grazing in?

Only you can (and should) decide!

Mistake Number 3
Risking the Cow, Instead of the Milk

My Granddad grew up during the Depression. His generation knew what it meant to "lose it all". He and most of his buddies were bred to be a thrifty bunch. They learned that hard work, spending wisely, and saving what was left was the key to a Worry Free retirement. Of course, it didn't hurt matters that most of granddad's generation worked for companies providing pension plans (my grand-dad called it mailbox money).

So how did granddad's safe and secure notion of guaranteed "mailbox money" get put out to pasture? Why in the world would Americans ever leave the peaceful pastures of safety and security and begin following the herd into the world of risk and uncertainty by investing their hard-earned retirement savings in things like growth mutual funds (with the result for some – plunging over the cliff)?

To understand the gradual disappearance of Granddad's "mailbox money," we need to back up to 1978, the year a room full of politicians got together and passed into law one of the goofiest ideas of them all; a law that would forever change the retirement landscape of guaranteed mailbox money. It was called the *Revenue Act of 1978.*

Today, most Americans know of this act simply as the 401(k) Plan.

Without boring you with the details of how this tax code took effect (tax laws are like a good steak – the steak looks good sizzling on your plate until you consider the details of Chuck's Slaughterhouse and how it got there – not quite as appetizing. Anyway, this new law allowed corporations to chuck their high-priced pension plans, and replace them with no obligation (on their part) 401k plans. In other words, the obligation to fend for one's retirement fell on one's self.* (See page 142)

"But Tony," you say again, "everybody else says to always "max-out" my 401(k) plan. If the 401(k) is not guaranteed like the pension plan, who is responsible for convincing millions of Americans to follow the herd?"

In my opinion: Wally World!

In 1980 there were approximately 564 mutual funds offered by Wally World. Notice the number of pension plans in 1980 as compared to the number of 401(k) plans during that same time period: 148,096 pension plans and only ten 401(k) plans offered by Employers. Also notice the amount of money managed by these funds: $134.7

YEAR	NUMBER OF PENSIONS	NUMBER OF 401(k) PLANS	NUMBER OF MUTUAL FUNDS & ASSETS (in billions of $)
1980	148,096	10	Approx. 134 Billion
1990	113,062	97,614	Approx. 1 Trillion
2000	48,773	348,053	Approx. 7 Trillion
2007	48,982	490,917	Approx. 12 Trillion

SOURCES: Private Pension Plan Bulletin Historical Tables and Graphs. US Department of Labor, Employee Benefits Security Administration. February 2009.

2009 Investment Company Fact Book 49th Edition. By the Investment Company Institute. Copyright 2009.

billion dollars. I know, that sounds like a lot of money, but in the scheme of the entire economy, it's chump change.

Over this period of time, Trillions of dollars (that's trillions with a T) moved from the guaranteed pension plans into the world of mutual funds. Notice that as more and more 401(k) plans hit the streets two things happened: first, the number of pension plans decreased and secondly, the number of growth and mutual funds skyrockets.

Just a coincidence you say? I don't think so!

The result for all parties involved:

1. Today, Joe's 401(k) resembles a 201(k).

2. Unlike Granddad, Americans go to bed at night without Sleep Insurance.

3. Employers no longer have any skin in the game.

4. Wally has his brand on millions of Americans

by controlling TRILLIONS of dollars in these so-called "conservative" mutual funds.

5. Uncle Sam? He doesn't care. He's patiently waiting for Wally to bring folks to the slaughterhouse [that's the time in your life when you go to try to spend your 401(k) and the tax laws written by the politicians butcher your cow as they carve out all the taxes you owe them].

"But Tony, all this is enlightening, but it doesn't help me! I'm the person whose 401(k) looks more like a 201(k), while the hired help representing my employer's 401(k) plan keeps banging on the milk bucket of "hang in there" and "don't run away."

There is a solution to this problem. Let me explain with another story.

There once lived a farmer, who was well-known in the small community in which he and his wife lived, who suffered from a common condition among farmers in the area known as "Big Hat – No Cattle."

To the rest of the farming community, the farmer was doing well. But he knew better. He, along with his wife, had spent money they didn't have, to buy things they really didn't need, only in an attempt to impress people they didn't much like anyway. Unless something miraculous happened (and happened quickly), the farmer and his wife would soon find themselves in The Poor House.

One sunny morning, upon proceeding to the barn to milk their one and only cow, Betsy, the farmer noticed that the milk proceeding from Betsy's udder was not white, but gold! Startled, the farmer picked up the milk bucket full of the golden liquid and raced to the farmhouse, shouting the good news to his wife.

"Honey, Betsy's milk is pure gold!"

So they loaded up the truck and moved to Beverly (wait, that's another story...sorry). So the farmer and his wife carefully transferred the golden substance from the milk bucket to a glass jar and drove their dilapidated pickup to the goldsmith located in the big city.

After a few quick tests, the Goldsmith confirmed that the golden substance produced by Betsy was indeed pure gold. The Goldsmith quickly took the glass jar of gold and gave Farmer Brown $1,000!

"Whoo-hooo!" shouts the farmer. "We're rich!"

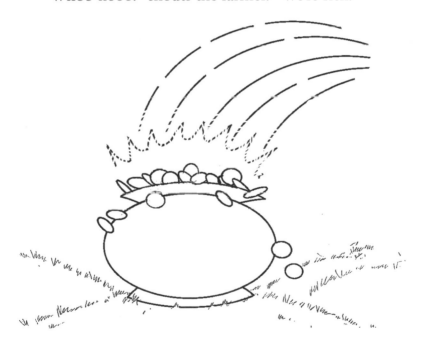

The next morning, the farmer skipped his routine of breakfast and hurried to the barn to milk ole' Betsy. Once again, Betsy produced enough golden milk to fill another bucket. For several weeks, the routine of milking the gold from Betsy continued as the farmer traded in the golden substance for cold hard cash, which always seemed to find its way off the farm as he and his wife continued to purchase bigger and better hats (gadgets and gismos).

One day, much to the farmer's surprise, Betsy produces only enough of the golden milk to fill half the milk bucket. For the next several weeks, Betsy's golden milk production decreases even more. The farmer grows anxious as his golden stream of income fades away. You see, the farmer has fallen into the trap of ratcheting up his lifestyle to match his income. It's like the old saying goes: "a luxury once enjoyed, soon becomes a necessity."

Farmer Brown couldn't let this happen.

So the next morning, instead of his usual routine of milking Betsy, Farmer Brown (reasoning that he needed to find the true source of Betsy's golden milk) herded Betsy into his new truck and trailer for her final destination at Chuck's Slaughterhouse. If only he could find all the gold at once, Farmer Brown would be rich overnight.

I guess you know the rest of the story. Without Betsy (the real "source" of the milk), the golden milk (income) stopped. It was over.

So Tony, you ask, what in the world does this have to do with my money?

Everything!

You see, most people forget that there must be a "source" – a Betsy if you will – that one can count on to produce a regular flow of income (the milk). The key to a worry free retirement is not putting the source at risk. Because if you do, you're likely to get slaughtered.

So here's my question: if there was a simple way to

guarantee that your cow (your savings and investments) AND your milk (the income you need to live on) would last a lifetime, would you want to know about it?

Yes, you say?

Good news! There is a relatively new (ingenious if you ask me) financial tool that allows you and I to do just that. The product: a Fixed Index Annuity (FIA).

This unique concept, introduced in the late '90s by a handful of insurance companies, is quickly gaining recognition as one of the safest, least costly (in the way of fees and taxes) and most predictable retirement planning tools available.

A Fixed Index Annuity (FIA) gives savers and investors alike, the opportunity to "participate" in the stock market without ever putting their principal at risk (see illustration below).

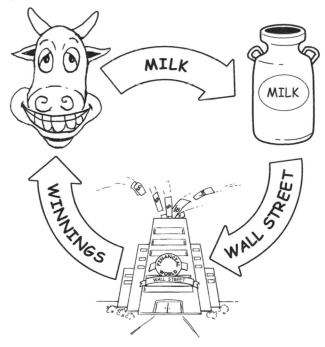

Key concept for safety: "participate in the stock market vs. investing in the stock market." See how the FIA behaved over the past 10 years compared to the roller coaster ride of the stock market (as represented here by the S&P 500). Notice, as the stock market goes up, the FIA goes up (as a percent of the overall market as well). When the market tanks, the FIA locks in the value so you cannot lose what you just made.

Now that's what I call Sleep Insurance!

"But Tony," you respond. "Why doesn't Wall Street offer these products?"

I'm not sure unless (my opinion here is purely speculative as to why they don't sell them) Wall Street feels they can't make enough money selling them (these products don't pay the hired help a recurring fee, just a one time commission). Unlike products offered by Wall Street, the FIA is not a "transaction" product but a retirement plan-

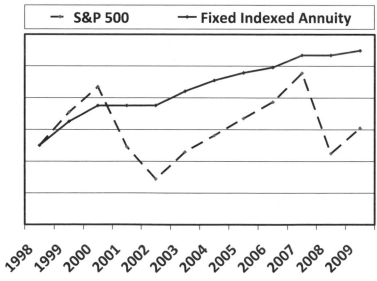

Disclaimer: The above graph plots historical performance of the S&P 500 for the years indicated and how a typical indexed annuity with annual reset would perform during that same time period. This does not guarantee future performance.

ning vehicle whereby you put your money in and basically leave it alone until such time as you're ready to start your mailbox money. With an FIA, there is nothing to "transact" so there is no reason to charge ongoing fees, which does not fit Wall Street's business model.

Another reason Wall Street doesn't sell them is that currently, the FIA is not considered a security, but rather an insurance product. Securities are registered and regulated by a government body known as the Securities and Exchange Commission (SEC). Stocks, bonds, mutual funds, and the like, are "securities" products, not insurance products.

By the way, back in my money management days of the 90's (yes, I used to follow and believe everything Wall Street told me, too) the FIA did not appeal to me. That's because I wanted (like Farmer Brown) all the market would give me and my clients. I wasn't interested in "participating" in the market. Now, I know better.

Will you get rich quick with an FIA? No, but neither will you end up in The Poor House. Moral to the story: If you don't like the thought of crying over spilt milk, don't put Betsy at risk. Keep her safe.

Mistake Number 4
Stockpiling Hay For Everyone Else But You

I'm sure you've heard of the Bible's Golden Rule: "Do unto others as you'd have others do unto you." But did you realize that the Financial World has their own Golden Rule? It says: "He who makes the rules, gets the gold (OPM)!"

To understand how the Financial World is so successful at attracting OPM, we must first learn the rules that they play by. On the next page are the four Financial Worlds and how they make money.

Financial Institution	How They Survive	What They Promise	What You Get
Government	Taxes	More Hope	More Inflation
Wall Street	Fees/Commissions	More Growth	More Risk
Insurance Companies	Premiums	More Protection	More LOC
Banks	Fees/Interest	More Stuff	More Debt

Still confused? Think of it this way: remember the character, Dracula? In order to survive, Dracula needed what? Blood, right? Without it, he would die. The Financial World is a lot like Dracula. They need money (OPM). Without it, they will die.

It's that simple.

In working in the trenches with thousands of people over the years, I've noticed that while many people have a game plan for "saving and investing" money (it's called the "accumulation phase" of life), those same folks do not have a game plan for "using and enjoying" it (the *"spending phase"*). That's because the Financial World takes ownership (I like to think of it as "branding" with their logo) of our money.

Don't believe me? Try this little experiment with your favorite Financial Institution; pick up the phone and politely inform them to liquidate (take your cow and go home) your account and send you a check, TODAY. Then, listen to their reaction. More than likely, they will go into panic mode and if need be, bring in the hired guns to try to convince you to not take it from them. Forget the fact that this is your money and you can do whatever you want with it. This money is YOUR money. Sometimes, we have to remind them of that.

Oh, and speaking of the Bible's Golden Rule, there's a ton of other truths about money and possessions within the pages of the world's best-selling book. One of my favorite sections of the Bible is the book of Ecclesiastes. Talk about stockpiling a lot of hay in your barn. The billionaire who wrote this book describes the vanity (meaninglessness) of stockpiling money all your life, only to realize that at the end of the day (when you kick the bucket) it's all going to someone who will more than likely squander it!

That's not the road I want to end up on, but it can happen to any of us: we work and worry ourselves sick about stockpiling more and more hay, and for what? To leave it to someone who'll probably blow it.

Don't get me wrong, I honestly believe there is nothing wrong with stockpiling money for the future, unless it takes control of our lives and zaps our joy in the process. Moral to the story: at some point, you either decide to spend it on yourselves and those whom you care about (family and charity) or let others spend it for you (the government, insurance companies, Wall Street, banks, favorite attorney, relatives you never really cared for, nursing home, etc.).

So now that we've reviewed God's Golden Rule and the Golden Rule of the Financial World, what's yours? What should YOUR "Golden Rule" be when it comes to using and enjoying your money?

Depending on your age, here are two financial products that much of the herd doesn't follow, but upon learning the truth, can help you certainly gain more control over your money.

Dividend Participating Whole Life (DPWL), or Whole Life as it is more commonly referred to.

The wealthy fellow referred to in Ecclesiastes would have loved Whole Life Insurance because Whole Life (DPWL) is one of the few (if not only) financial products that provides both tax-free access to cash (for anything we want) during our lifetime and a barn full of tax-free, cold hard cash for our loved ones when we kick the bucket. While this product is for all ages, it works very well for young folks.

Take my son Phillip.

At age 23, Phillip graduated college and landed a full time job. To help him save more money, reduce taxes over time and provide himself a source of accessible, safe money, I convinced Phillip to invest $500 a month into his very own Whole Life policy. Sure, I had to twist his arm (keep in mind, for a 23-year-old right out of college, 500 bucks a month is a lot of milk money) but over the long haul he will grow to appreciate the fact that he is not putting his money at risk nor wasting money with term life insurance and unnecessary taxes and LOC.

{By the way, to learn the truth about Whole Life, please meet with someone who understands all the details of Whole Life! Most of the hired help tossing cow dung on it have no clue how this product really works. You're going to have to learn from someone that understands it.}

Below is Phillip's actual whole life policy illustration

showing the "non-guaranteed" values based on "current dividends" (dividends are not guaranteed but are as low as I've ever seen them, so in my estimation, should pan out).

Dividend Participating Whole Life
(Non-guaranteed Current Dividend Scale)

Age	Year	Premium	Cash Value	Death Benefit
23	1	$6,000	$3,997	$340,738
25	3	$6,000	$12,713	$410,874
30	8	$6,000	$47,369	$578,477
35	13	$6,000	$93,992	$735,869
40	18	$6,000	$155,377	$887,361
45	23	$6,000	$235,898	$1,039,452
50	28	$6,000	$341,061	$1,197,730
55	33	$6,000	$478,416	$1,366,019
60	38	$6,000	$655,902	$1,555,074
65	43	$6,000	$883,743	$1,774,275

This illustration has been prepared using current dividend scale. Illustration is also subject to underwriting. This illustration assumes that the current illustrated, non-guaranteed elements will continue unchanged for all years shown. Actual results may be more or less favorable than those shown.

When Phillip reaches age 65, based on current dividends, his cash value (that's the money that's available to him during his lifetime) is $883,743 while the death benefit (the amount of tax free cash that goes to his loved ones when he kicks the bucket) is $1,774,275.

"But Wait...as they say on late night TV...there's more!"

Through a special rider called "waiver of premium for disability," should Phillip become totally disabled the insurance company will continue to pay the $500 a month (for as long as Phillip remains disabled). Try calling your 401(k) plan administrator and ask them if they'll do this... of course not!

The Split Annuity Concept

Here's another safe idea for using and enjoying more of your money that's very appropriate for folks at or near retirement; the Split Annuity. Take a look…

Person A is a typical retiree I meet who has $200,000 in a CD currently earning 3%. Their main objective is to protect principal and live off the interest. This was a good strategy when CD's were paying 5 or 6%, but 3%?

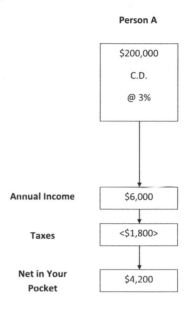

Notice the retiree in the CD strategy receives $6,000 per year. However, Uncle Sam gets to take his fair share in taxes from the $6,000 (here's where paying taxes on the same dollar more than once comes into play). So let's say this person is in a 30% tax bracket. For the privilege of being an American citizen, the IRS takes $1,800 (30% of $6,000—I know, this doesn't seem fair, but it is the law). This leaves person A with a "net" annual income of only $4,200.

Person B takes the same $200,000, and instead of giving it to the bank, he or she gives it to the insurance company. The insurance company "splits" the money into two separate buckets: one is what's known as an "immediate annuity" and the other a "fixed annuity" (more on these products later).

Split Annuity Concept

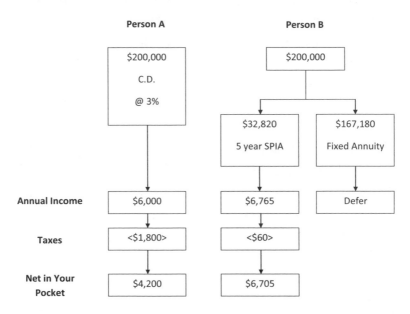

With the split annuity, the annual income is $6,765 a year. Plus, based on a favorable provision in the tax law (called an exclusion ratio) our retiree only pays taxes on $202, providing a higher net annual income of $2,505.

"But Tony," you say, "isn't Person A draining one of the buckets down to nothing?"

Great question!

The first bucket under the Split Annuity strategy pays out more money (principal plus interest) so that the retiree can safely use and enjoy more money (which is the whole point). When the first bucket is completely empty, we simply move over and tap into the second bucket which, during the period of time that the first bucket is being drained, has all grown "tax-deferred" (no taxes during accumulation, thus no LOC). So with the Split Annuity, you get more income, pay less taxes and Sleep Insurance, all in one!

Pretty neat, huh?

Mistake Number 5
No Game Plan for Using and Enjoying 401(k) and IRA, and other Retirement Accounts

For most Americans, the 401(k) is their most valuable asset for retirement. By the way, confusing governmental terms and acronyms such as IRA, 457, 403b, SEPIRA, Thrift Plan, etc. all behave just like the 401k. These "qualified" plans have buried within them, the now infamous "tax tumor." So now that we know about the tax-tumor, what are our options for dealing with it?

On the next page is a 401(k) worth $300,000. Assuming we lived in a perfect world (no taxes on the 401(k) when we go to take money out), we'd have all the $300,000 to use and enjoy. Unfortunately, we've got to deal with our "progressive" tax system that allows the government to take their fair share first (pre-tax really means you're just postponing the tax).

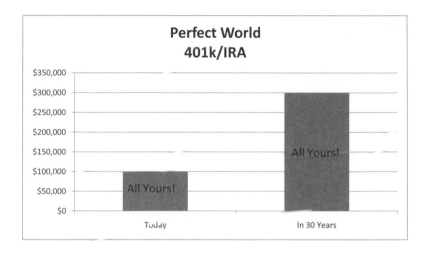

So there's the government's share...bigger than life. The question: what are you going to do about it? Here are your only options:

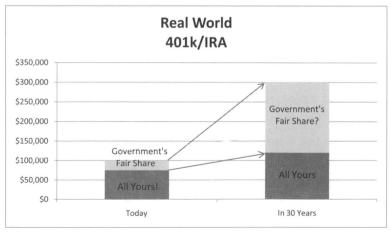

1. Ignore It. Imagine your doctor discovering a malignant tumor within your body. You could ignore it, but if you do, all the tumor is going to do is grow and get worse. You could do the same with your tax infested 401(k) or IRA, just pretend the tax tumor doesn't exist and pray the next President of hope and change will demand Congress repeal the tax law and give you the 401(k) tax-free (this would be a miracle!).

2. Spend It. Yes, I said spend it. I realize the Financial World told you not to, but if you don't spend it, Uncle Sam will get his fair share at some point anyway. And at what tax rate? If you're like me, and believe taxes will increase, spending it starts sounding even better. Bigger barns don't always mean more money in your pocket.

3. Stretch It. The CPA's and technical folks love this option because they contend that the government is "letting" you defer the taxes. True, but what if tax rates do go up in the future? And what about inflation—if you keep deferring these dollars off into the future, what will they be worth? This idea of deferring the taxes and only taking "minimum distributions" (is getting the minimum why you worked so hard to save money—not to me) for the rest of your life and that of your heirs, makes me wonder if deferring the enjoyment of the money is all that it's cracked up to be. As I see it, this strategy never allows you to eat and enjoy the cow. It's only promising you a little cream off the top while the Financial World gets to use and enjoy the whole thing.

4. Insure it. Assuming we can agree that everyone's going to die, why in the world would anyone NOT own some amount of tax-free "Whole Life" life insurance. In

most cases, this is the only way to guarantee tax free money to replace the tax that will surely be due at death on the 401(k) plan (unless your beneficiaries stretch it).

But, Tony, all the folks on radio and TV tell me to buy term life insurance…isn't term much cheaper than whole life? In the words of Farmer Brown: "term life insurance is like wettin' the bed…it feels pretty good at first, but sooner or later, somebody's gotta change the sheets!"

Term life insurance is so cheap because the insurance companies know that you and your family will (more than likely) never collect on it. That's because just about the time we're ready to die (when we're old and gray), the premiums get so high we can't afford it (what a deal).

Remember, life insurance is the only asset that guarantees a certain amount of cold-hard "tax-free" cash when you need it, and not a minute too late when it comes to kicking the bucket. And "tax-free" beats "taxes" every time.

5. Convert it. This is when you take the taxable cow (your existing IRA) and magically turn it into a tax-free cow. The process is called a Roth Conversion and any retirement specialist that knows anything about 401(k)/IRA's will be able to help you with this. Keep in mind that when and if you do convert a traditional IRA to a Roth IRA, Uncle Sam will want his taxes right then and there. Look before you leap!

In summary, the tax tumor buried in your 401(k) must be dealt with. To get it out will be painful. You can pay Uncle Sam now, or pay him later; he really doesn't care. The government will one day get their fair share. Your responsibility is to learn your options in order to give you and your family the best chance for keeping as much of your hard-earned money as possible. That's why it is so important to work with a retirement specialist trained in this area (most advisors aren't).

As Farmer Brown always says, "why pay taxes if you don't have to?"

Mistake Number 6
Leaving your cow in the wrong stall

This mistake is a tough one to relate to cows. I thought about taking advantage of our illustration of the Bull and the Cow, but decided it might get a tad too graphic. So since this book promises to maintain its theme on cows and money, I'm going to fall back to the story of Farmer Brown and the parking garage.

One day, Farmer Brown was summoned by the big city Courthouse for Jury duty. Rarely did Farmer Brown ever go to the "big city" and never had he actually driven the confusing one-way streets of downtown where the Courthouse was located. Farmer Brown would have to navigate the highways and byways of the big city and worst of all, find a place to park.

After several hours of driving, Farmer Brown finally arrives downtown. Upon locating the courthouse for Jury duty, Farmer Brown began the daunting task of finding a place to park his beat up pick up truck. Upon turning off the busy one-way street and into one of the many parking garages, much to his amazement, at this particular garage, no one was available to take his money.

Instead, located at the main entrance was a small box with a green button attached to a stand with a bright green button which Farmer Brown proceeded to push.

After pulling his parking ticket from the box, Farmer Brown proceeds into the parking garage to find a place to park.

"Free parking," thought Farmer Brown. "What a wonderful surprise!"

After eight hours of jury duty, Farmer Brown decides to do some shopping for Mrs. Brown. "What the heck," he thought, "especially since parking in the garage is free!"

It was nearly 9:00 pm when Farmer Brown located his truck in the parking garage. Slowly making his way toward the exit, he notices a man in a booth with a gate blocking the exit. As Farmer Brown pulls his truck to the booth, the man in the booth abruptly holds out his hand and eyes Farmer Brown.

"Whatcha need, Tiger," asks Farmer Brown?

"I need your ticket," responds the attendant.

"What ticket?" exclaims the perplexed Farmer.

"The one you got from the little box when you drove

into the garage," a now somewhat agitated attendant responds.

Farmer Brown hands the ticket to the attendant.

"That'll be twenty-four dollars," says the attendant.

"Twenty-four dollars!" responds a surprised Farmer.

"Sorry," quips the attendant, "the longer you stay, the more you pay."

What I just described to you is a "Traditional" IRA (or any other "pre-tax" retirement account). Basically, the Traditional IRA leads you to "believe" that your stay in the parking garage is free (the government doesn't ask for their taxes up front – that's why they call your contributions "pre-tax"). And don't expect the man in the booth to accept anything less than his fair share.

Certainly, you can stay in the parking garage as long as you want. Unfortunately, the longer you stay (leave your money in the pre-tax account) the worse it gets. This would be a good time to go back over the stuff on the tax tumor discussed earlier.

The next day, Farmer Brown returns to the big city for his second round of jury duty. Frustrated over the rate charged by yesterday's parking attendant, Farmer Brown pulls his pickup truck into a different parking garage hoping to negotiate a different fee with the attendant. As Farmer Brown rounds the corner of the entrance, he quickly notices that this parking garage is different. It has a booth with an attendant located at the entrance. As the Farmer approaches, the man in the booth sticks his hand out. Confused by this new arrangement, the Farmer stops his truck to find out more.

"Whatcha' need Tiger?" asks Farmer Brown.

"Twenty-four dollars," quips the attendant.

"Twenty-four dollars!" responds a slightly shocked Farmer Brown. "The last garage didn't charge me 'till I left the garage."

"Oh," says the attendant. "You must have parked in the "pre-tax" garage. This is the "after-tax" garage," says the attendant matter of factly."

"Why would I want to pay twenty-four dollars now?" the Farmer asks.

"If you pay me up front, you won't have to pay me later. In fact, I'll let you park in here for as long as you want!" states the attendant.

"You mean to tell me that if in' I park here for 20 days, the rate is still only twenty-four bucks?" a surprised Farmer asks.

"You got it," the attendant says.

The second parking garage Farmer Brown parked in describes the Roth IRA. Unlike the "pre-tax" Traditional IRA, the ROTH IRA allows you to save money that has already been taxed—called "after-tax" money. The benefit to you is that by paying the toll up front, from that point forward, all of the earnings and income will be tax-free forever!!!

So for everyone who is eligible (sorry, if you make too much money or don't have any "earned" income, the government discriminates against you) the Roth IRA is something you should most definitely consider. And, take it from someone who is in the retirement planning field: knowing that the taxes are no longer an issue when you take money out of the Roth (exit the garage without having to pay the toll) makes planning for retirement a heck of a lot easier.

Mistake Number 7
No Mailbox Money During Retirement

Remember our earlier discussion about Granddad and his guaranteed lifetime income—what he called "mailbox money"? My thoughts: if mailbox money was good enough for granddad, it should be good enough for us.

With pension plans going the way of the cattle prod, a retirement plan that includes a predictable stream of income for the rest of our lives is a no-brainer. And speaking from experience, I can tell you that there is only ONE financial tool that can accomplish this:

The Annuity!

"But Tony," you say, "the Financial World keeps banging on the milk bucket of 'max out my 401k plan, invest in growth mutual funds, buy term life insurance and invest the difference'…I never hear anything positive about annuities!" To which I would reply, just because everybody's telling you to follow the herd doesn't mean YOU should.

Over the years, I've worked on both sides of the aisle – with Wall Street and with insurance companies. And regardless of what either side is preaching, at some point, the majority of retirees "must" have a guaranteed source of mailbox money. It's that simple.

While annuities have been around for over a century, there is nevertheless a ton of misinformation about them, unfortunately flowing from writers, advisors, and pundits who lack understanding of the entire retirement planning process and the need for a guaranteed stream of income that one can never outlive.

So as someone who personally works with these products on a daily basis, please allow me to share the truth about these wonderful products and some of the common misconceptions you keep hearing about.

{By the way, the problem with following the herd is that some of the people giving advice are not in the trenches every day looking into the lives of every day people who are worried sick about their money and how to safeguard and protect it.}

Misconception #1:
Annuities come with huge surrender penalties.

Surrender penalties are nothing more than a "penalty for early withdrawal". It is there to not only protect the annuitant (the title given to the person placing their money—premium—with an insurance company annuity) but also to protect the insurance company. Let's face it, the last thing you need to worry about is the insurance company going belly-up. The more the insurance company is willing to promise (interest rate, income, etc.) the longer you're going to have to leave the money with them to avoid surrender charges. Surrender penalties within the annuity allow the insurance company to protect themselves from people making a run on the company, thus guaranteeing that your annuity is safe and secure and the insurance company can continue to meet the contractual obligations made to their annuitants.

Holding onto your money and putting a penalty for early withdrawal is nothing new; banks do it all the time. Just take a look at CD rates: the longer the maturity, the higher the interest they pay for your money. However, with these higher rates comes the possibility of higher surrender penalties to you if you get out early.

Misconception #2:
All annuities charge high fees.

Nothing could be further from the truth unless you are referring to Variable Annuities. Variable annuities, which are sold mainly by Wall Street, are mutual funds in an annuity wrapper. The reason Variable Annuities charge higher fees (as opposed to fixed annuities) is due to the risk of the stock market within them.** (See page 142). While a Variable Annuity can make huge returns (based on the success of the market) it requires the insurance company issuing them to charge fees in case things don't pan out (the market crashes and you want to guarantee either a lifetime income and/or something for your family when you die).

Fixed Annuities on the other hand, are not invested in the stock market but instead invest in portfolios of safer instruments like corporate and government bonds. The insurance company issuing fixed annuities makes their money (profit) on the spread between their overall bond portfolio and what they can pay you on the balance after deducting their expenses.

Misconception #3:
Annuities are difficult to understand.

I am often amused at the various articles filled with misinformation regarding annuities (obviously written by people who have little understanding of annuities and/or too lazy to take the time to read the contracts and learn the field of retirement planning) as they go on-and-on about the complexities of annuities; to which I'd reply: "If you don't understand annuities stop wasting your time and ours by writing about them."

Can you imagine a minister telling you not to read (or believe in) the Good Book because it is too complex? I confess that my knowledge of how a TV works is pretty limited, but that doesn't keep me from watching my favorite programs.

Regardless of whether you're 25 or 75, if you are looking for an investment that will give you guaranteed mailbox money in retirement, I encourage you – strongly research and consider an annuity. For retirement minded folks who are more concerned about the return "of" their money AND a guaranteed return "on" it, it is the way to go.

Misconception #4:
With an annuity, my money is tied up.

While the vast majority of annuities come with surrender penalties, most still offer flexible ways to "untie" your money so you can use it. Here's a few:

1. Beginning after the first month of the contract, you can request the insurance company send you the interest earned;

2. After the first full contract year, you can request 10%—without penalty—of the entire contract value, each and every year. In some annuities if you skip taking the 10% one year, you can take 20% the following year;

3. If you are diagnosed with a terminal illness or go into a nursing home, most will allow you to take out more than 10% penalty free each year;

4. Upon your death, the full value of the annuity will be paid to anyone you choose, with no penalty whatsoever;

5. At the end of the surrender term (usually 5 to 16 years) you can cash out the entire annuity value at no penalty whatsoever;

6. You can annuitize (usually at any time) and begin receiving a lifetime monthly income without penalty;

7. If your annuity contract has a "guaranteed lifetime income rider" you can begin monthly income payments when you choose and even change your mind later and take the remaining annuity value in a lump-sum cash pay-

ment (newer feature which differs from annuitization);

8.   And finally, you can "cash out" your annuity at any time if you're willing to deal with the surrender penalty. Of course, if you cash out the annuity after the surrender penalty expires, no problem getting all your money back (unless you are in a Variable Annuity and then, your account value could be less than you put in based on the market value).

So, as we can see, the right type of annuity is very, very flexible and accessible at any time as long as you use it appropriately.

Misconception #5:
Nothing is left for my family when I die.

Each week, I answer retirement planning questions on a morning TV call in show that is broadcast to over 600,000 households. We get lots of calls and questions on a wide variety of topics, but every once in awhile, I'll get calls about annuities, like this one:

CALLER: Hi Tony, this is Linda calling from Louisville. I heard you say that annuities can be good retirement vehicles, but I don't like them!

TONY: May I ask why, Linda?

CALLER: Well, my mom, (by the tone of her voice, Linda doesn't sound like a happy-camper) who recently passed away, had an annuity that was paying her $800 a month...

TONY: (interrupts)...we call that mailbox money Linda...

CALLER: Yeah, whatever...any way, after she died, your so-called mailbox money stopped. And when I called the Insurance Company they said that she had annuitized the annuity – whatever the heck that means – on a life only basis. What are they talking about and why would mom ever do that?

TONY: Linda, may I ask you what other income your mother lived on?

CALLER: Well, she got social security of a thousand dollars a month and a couple hundred dollars in CD interest. Other than that, I guess that was about it.

TONY: Let me ask you a question Linda, can you live on $2,000 a month?

CALLER: Of course not.

TONY: Linda, your mother probably selected the "life only" option because she needed the highest income possible. The "life only", as opposed to other options with annuities that offer a survivor option upon death, meant that the insurance company had to guarantee her a lifetime income she couldn't outlive at the highest payout possible.

CALLER: Wait a minute; (Linda sounds as though she is having an ah-ha moment) are you telling me that if mom had lived 30 more years, the Insurance Company would have still "guaranteed" mom the $800 every month?

TONY: That's right.

CALLER: Her bank wouldn't do that. In fact, mom always fussed about having to drive around town chasing down the highest CD rates and how piddly the CD income was since most of them were only paying her 2%. I guess the annuity was pretty good after all, huh?

TONY: Sounds like she selected the right product for

her. And Linda, now knowing that your mother had a guaranteed income—even though you didn't get anything at her death—isn't that what you, as her daughter, would have wanted for your mother?

CALLER: Well sure, I only wanted mom to use and enjoy her money. Thanks, Tony (Linda now sounds like a happy-camper).

In the above example, Linda's mom "annuitized" her annuity. And since she elected the "life only" (this is the same option given to retirees who have had the luxury of a employer sponsored pension plan) upon her death, nothing would be left to her family. You can do the same thing with most annuities... and only an annuity—not a stock, bond, mutual fund or other non-annuity investment—has this feature.

So if you DO NOT annuitize the annuity, your family is assured of getting what remains of the annuity at your death (unless of course, you simply take withdrawals during your lifetime or surrender the annuity and do something else with it—which you can certainly do).

Misconception #6:
The different types of annuities are confusing.

Don't let all the different types of annuities confuse you. They basically come in four flavors:

a.) <u>Fixed Interest Rate Annuity</u> is a contract whereby you give your money to an insurance company and are guaranteed a fixed, set rate of interest for one or more years. What they pay you is generally based on the return of the insurance company's investment portfolio, but you get the guaranteed rate regardless of their profitability or loss. Does this sound similar to the way a bank CD works?

b.) <u>Variable Annuity</u>. Insurance Company invests the money you give them into mutual funds or some other type of security. While you have unlimited upside potential and can make a lot of money in a variable annuity, you also have unlimited downside and can lose a lot of money. In fact, over the past several years, you might have experienced or seen market losses. I have personally witnessed variable annuity losses of up to 50%! Such losses were no doubt by some people who, in many cases, could ill afford to lose that much of their retirement savings. That's the main reason the Variable Annuity tends to charge higher fees – it is the only way to protect the insurance company from potential losses the market might suffer (remember, the insurance company has a contractual obligation to not only protect O.P.M. but also turn a profit).

c.) <u>Fixed Indexed Annuity</u>. During my money management days of the go-go '90s, I remember insurance companies calling on me to sell these products. At that time, with many of my clients making huge returns in the stock market, I had no interest in selling these products. Why? Because they limit, cap or participate in the stock market. Of course, that's why they are so safe—because your money is not actually in the market. For a review of this, turn back to page 99 and read the story of the golden milk.

Key point to remember about Fixed Index Annuities is that when the stock market goes up, you generally get some of the gains. But when the market tanks, you lose nothing and the gains you made the prior year are not lost!

It is a really good deal when you think about it, especially if you're a risk adverse saver who doesn't like losing money. This comparison of the variable annuity and the fixed indexed annuity is like the tale of the tortoise and the hare—fast starts and abrupt stops may not be as good as always moving forward at a steady pace.

d.) <u>Immediate Annuity</u>. The ultimate form of mailbox money, you invest your money (technically a premium) to an insurance company in exchange for a lifetime income for a set number of years (called a period certain), for the rest of your life only (called a life only option) or for your life and the life of a named beneficiary (referred to as joint and survivor option). While the concept of guaranteed mailbox money for the rest of a set term or one's life sounds good, there is one drawback: once you tell the insurance company to send you income, you cannot change the election.

Example: needing as much income as you can get your hands on, you elect the "life only" option of your annuity which guarantees that the monthly income you will be receiving will last for the rest of "your" life. But what if you need a lump sum from the annuity (maybe an emergency comes up)? Basically, you're out of luck! That's because once the immediate annuity income option is elected (you turn on the mailbox money) you cannot change it.

So before ever establishing an immediate income, be certain you are okay with the option elected because you cannot change it down the road.

{Surprisingly, we see the concept of the Immediate Annuity used over at the Local Lottery Office (poor man's tax collection service is what Farmer Brown called the Lottery). Notice how the lottery winner gets two options for taking the money: lump sum (all at once and less than advertised) or a guaranteed income (mailbox money) stream for a certain number of years (annuitization). So there you have it…even the Government believes in the concept of annuities!}

Misconception #7:
Annuities are bad for older folks.

Most of the older folks I work with and meet are looking for two things: 1) safety of their money, 2) not running out of it!

This misconception makes no sense unless the older person IS NOT looking for safety and security, and assuming the older person is looking at a Fixed Annuity (as opposed to a Variable Annuity which contains more risk and higher fees).

Again, without beating a dead cow, the majority of annuities (mainly the fixed variety) are very well suited to the older retiree. That's because the annuity not only guarantees the return of the money, but also guarantees a certain amount of mailbox money. What's not for older folks to like about that?

Misconception #8:
Annuities aren't safe.

Now if you are talking about comparing them to FDIC insured bank products, annuities are not FDIC insured and are not backed by the federal government. They are backed by the same insurance companies that protect your house, car, life, health and virtually everything else of value. A review of the factual history of fixed annuities shows that they are very safe. I have worked with insurance companies for over twenty-five years and have never had a problem with any annuity contract. In fact, during the Great Depression, there is no history or record of any insurance companies failing to pay claims on their contracts. This period was the most turbulent time of our country's history. Pretty good track record, wouldn't you say?

Still, it would be good for you to check with your State Department of Insurance (the government agency that regulates insurance companies) to confirm something called the State Guarantee Association Fund. Your state's guaranty fund was established to protect citizens holding annuities and other insurance policies. Of course, just like FDIC dollar limits, these funds do have limits that vary by state. Rather than going into detail here, I would simply suggest that you contact your State Department of Insurance to clarify how this insurance program works in your state.

Misconception #9:
Annuities pay huge commissions to agents.

Oh really? Who says, Wall Street?

Insurance Agents (the agent or advisor must hold an insurance license to sell any of the four types of annuities mentioned earlier) mainly live off commissions – a one-time reward paid to the Agent for bringing the insurance company OPM.

Years ago, the majority of hired help working for Wall Street earned commissions too; however, over the years, Wally has been herding consumers into other pastures that charge "fees" on accounts. And these fees usually last (charge you) a lifetime. Speaking from experience (I've been paid from both sides of the fee and commission aisle) I feel commissions are the way for consumers to go.

Take a look at a 50-year-old considering a Fixed Annuity with an Insurance Agent (agent will be paid a one-time commission) vs. putting the same amount of money into a growth mutual fund with Wall Street (Wall Street charge commissions up front, but always gathers fees each year based on the value of the account).

Comparison of Commissions vs. Fees

	Fixed Annuity	Wally World
Amount Invested	$100,000	$100,000
One-time Commission	($6,000)	($0)
Amount Left	$100,000	$100,000
Annual Fees	(0%)	(2%)
Future Value of Account	$324,340	$176,922
Paid to Agent	$6,000	Paid to Wally World $147,418

We'll assume Wall Street charges no up front commission but charges 2% per year in fees.

As you can see, with the Fixed Annuity (side A) even though the agent received a one-time commission from the insurance company of (let's say) 6% – or $6,000, the 50-year-old's entire $100,000 is working for them (assuming the contract is not surrendered during the surrender period). In other words, the hired help is paid by the insurance company, not directly by the investor!

With Wall Street (side B) your full $100,000 is working for you as well; and while Wally's hired help (there's two cowboys working with your account now—the advisor who has to charge a fee and the mutual fund manager who also charges a fee) does not take a commission, they do skim 2% off the top each and every year, regardless of whether your account goes up or down. Pretty predictable for them, not so predictable for you.

Moral to the story: whether it's a commission or a fee, the hired help has to get paid. The real question: is the hired help worth it? How much they get paid is sometimes determined by how much you're willing to give them. You do have a choice.

Misconception #10:
Annuities are good replacements for life insurance.

Just because annuities and life insurance are both contracts issued by insurance companies, it doesn't mean they are created equal. While the primary purpose of an annuity is income, life insurance is meant to provide "tax-free, cold-hard cash" upon death. In fact, the ideal scenario is to have a retirement game plan that includes both annuities AND life insurance.

Consider a retiree who, today, is the proud owner of a 401(k) (or IRA, 457, Thrift or any other "qualified" account) worth $300,000. (See page 115)

Is it all theirs?

Nope; because this is a "pre-tax" account—the government toll keeper is waiting for you when you exit the garage so he can collect his fair share—your taxes. Worst of all, since you aren't sure when you'll even leave the parking garage, it is now uncertain as to how much his "fair share" is going to be. If taxes go up in the future, he takes even more. Doesn't seem fair, does it?

You only have two options for avoiding (delaying the inevitable): 1) take less income now and continue to defer the taxes as long as you can, or 2) take more income now and pay Uncle Sam his share rather than putting off the pain!

You're "darned if you do, darned if you don't."

But what if you had both the $300,000 IRA/annuity and a $300,000 permanent (see why whole life makes sense now) life insurance policy that pays your beneficiaries $300,000 of cold hard, tax-free cash when you kick the bucket?

[Please quit listening to the rest of the herd saying you won't need life insurance in retirement. What I've discovered in working with so many retirees is that, in most cases, people wish they had more of it – not less of it.].

Moral of the story: while annuities may provide a cash balance to your heirs upon your death, or even have what is termed a "death benefit", the money is not passed tax-free. With an annuity, any money above your original premium (with an annuity, this is called your basis) will be taxed at ordinary income rates – just like a 401(k)/IRA. However, with life insurance, the money left to your family at death will go to them completely tax free, giving you the freedom to use and enjoy the rest of your money for the rest of your life.

Tony Wraps It Up

"**W**ell folks, that concludes our presentation, *The 7 Costly Mistakes People Make with Their Money, and How To Avoid Them*," says Tony as the crowd begins to close their workbooks. "I trust you now have a better understanding of how the Financial World operates and ideas to keep from following the herd.... Are there any comments?"

"Yes," says a young lady near the front row, "for the first time in my life I understand the difference between a Roth IRA and Traditional IRA."

"I know what I've learned," says another woman in the back of the room, "to look before I leap by learning to ask advisors the right questions and not just blindly follow their advice."

"Very good," responds Tony, "anyone else?"

An older gentleman seated in the middle of the room comments, "I now have a better understanding of annuities and why they are a great option for some of that mailbox money you keep talking about."

{As attendees gather up their belongings, a smartly dressed young man in the back of room, who up to this point has remained silent throughout Tony's presentation, slowly stands up and begins to speak.}

"Tony," says the young man as everyone stops to listen. "I'm a financial adviser – one of the hired hands from the Financial World you keep referring to," he says in a somewhat sarcastic voice.

"Great," exclaims Tony. "I'm glad you're here."

"Quite frankly," the young man continues, "when you first began your presentation, I was somewhat insulted by your comments about the Financial World – or Wally World as you put it," he says in a serious tone. "Yet," as the young man begins to relax a bit, "after listening to your entire presentation, it dawned on me that maybe you're not only referring to the tactics the Financial World uses to attract OPM."

"I like where you are going with this," smiles Tony. "Keep talking."

"I guess all you're really saying is that Wally World is not a place or a specific financial institution, but it is a "reality" – a Golden Rule the Financial World lives by in order to survive. But in the end, it is the responsibility of the consumer to create their own vision of what it is they want so that they can keep from following the herd," he says with confidence.

"Very good," continues Tony, "anything else you'll remember from tonight?"

"Yeah, there is," responds the young man as he begins to gather his things, "that cows are cows and people are people and from this point forward, I'll never confuse the two."

Tony smiles as the young man returns a smile.

The older gentleman in the front row slowly stands up and shouts, "Amen! Now let's get out of here...it's bedtime!"

Everyone laughs out loud.

Footnotes:

*For a great read on this subject, check out the wonderfully written book: "The Great 401(k) Hoax," by William Wolman & Anne Colamosca.

**For a great tool to determine what any insurance company is charging for their annuity, log on to www.TonyWalkerFinancial.com and click on the FREE ANNUITY FEE SHEET. Download this form and have the person selling the annuity fill it out, sign off on it and have them hand it back to you for your records.

Other Resources by Tony

1. TonyWalkerFinancial.com

2. 3Personalities.com

3. PerfectingYourWalk.com

4. GranddadsRetirement.com

"For the gate is small and the way is narrow that leads to life, and few are those who find it."

Matthew 7:14